THE HAYES BOOK OF
ADVENTURES

Patricia Howell

By
STEF DONEV
DAN MACKIE
J. TERRY WINIK

Editors:

NADIA PELOWICH
PAUL HAYES
CURTIS RUSH

Designed and Illustrated by
MARK HUGHES

DURKIN HAYES PUBLISHING LTD.
3312 Mainway, Burlington, Ontario L7M 1A7, Canada
One Colomba Drive, Niagara Falls, New York 14305, U.S.A.

Copyright © 1986 by Hayes Publishing Ltd. All rights reserved. No part of this book may be reproduced or transmitted in any form or by any means, electronic or mechanical, including photocopying, recording or by any information storage and retrieval system, without permission from the publisher.

ISBN 0-88625-093-5

Second Printing, 1992

CONTENTS

Float to Freedom 4
Glide 7
Solo Sail 8
Everest's First Woman 11
North Pole 12
Easier Ways to the Top 15
Double Eagle II 16
Treasure of Slot ter Hooge 19
In Search of the Yeti 20
Virunga's Mountain Gorillas 23
Heyerdahl's Tigris 24
South Pole 28
Robert Scott 31
Man on the Moon 32
Flying Machine 35
Family Trip 36
Through the Outback by Camel 39
Iran Escape 40
Entebbe 43
The Highest Ski Hill in the World ... 44
Deepest Dive 46

FLOAT TO FREEDOM

The Hutyra family lived in Czechoslovakia, inside miles of walls, barbed wire, mine fields and border guards. People of Czechoslovakia, a communist country, could not leave and enter as they pleased — that was part of the reason why Robert Hutyra wanted to escape and begin a new life somewhere else. If Hutyra and his family were caught trying to leave the country, however, they could be sent to prison, or even shot and killed! Since the border guards are used to people trying to escape, the Hutyras needed a good scheme to fool them.

Their plan: a hot-air balloon!

Hutyra could not just buy a hot-air balloon. Even if he could, the police would immediately suspect his plan. Instead, Hutyra and his wife had to make one . . . in secret. If they were found out by the police, prison awaited them!

Months were spent buying material, a little at a time from different stores, so their work would pass unsuspected. They decided to use nylon raincoats and pieces of rubberized cloth. The pieces were of many colors; when completed, their work would look like a great big patchwork quilt. They spent night after night in the attic, month after month, working secretly.

A lot had to be done. A propane burner to heat the air and so raise the balloon was also needed, and the gondola of the balloon (where the Hutyra family and a few of their possessions would ride) had to be built. Special considerations, such as bullet proofing the sides of the gondola with metal, could save their lives if the border guards tried to shoot them down as they were leaving.

At last, everything was completed and the wait began. Weather conditions had to be right.

On Wednesday, September 7, 1980, the wind was blowing in the direction they wanted — toward the neighboring country of Austria. The entire family — Robert, Jana, daughter Jana, Jr., and son Robert — loaded the balloon into the trunk of their car, took one last look at their home and at all of the belongings they would never see again, and drove to a deserted area near the border. Once there, they waited under cover of nightfall before starting to inflate the balloon.

Against the evening clouds, standing seven stories high, was their ride to freedom — if it worked! Imprisonment or death waited if it didn't. They climbed into the gondola and turned on the propane burners.

Up they shot!

But something went wrong! Down they came again with a crash!

On the way down, some tree branches ripped open the cloth in two jagged tears. Not only had they crashed, but they had crashed noisily. Had anyone heard them? Had the sound been reported? The police could already be on their way! They had to escape! Immediately!

They could not bother to repair the two tears in the balloon. They could only hope that the few minutes they had could allow them enough time to refill the air and that the leaks from the balloon would not be too severe. As their watches ticked, they prayed! With the family back on board the gondola, Robert started the burners to heat the air. They rose.

It was faster than they'd expected. Within seconds they were above the trees, and still climbing. But, suddenly there was a blaze of light! A searchlight had picked them out of the sky and was shining in Jana, Jr.'s face! They'd been spotted! The guards were shooting!

Higher and higher the balloon climbed until at last they were a mile up and beyond range of the communist guns.

For an hour they coasted through darkness, hoping, praying, never really sure if they were sailing across the border below. When their fuel was exhausted, they drifted to the ground.

But were they back in Czechoslovakia? Or could they really be in Austria? Were they free? Abandoning the balloon, they hid in the bushes, waiting. Each shared the same thought, "Did we make it?"

The noise of their landing had attracted attention. Soon they heard a car arrive. It stopped. People got out with flashlights, searching. Then, almost in disbelief, they heard what the searchers were saying: "Welcome to Austria!"

The Hutyras had risked all — and won!

GLIDE

Some ideas for movies come from real-life escapes. The idea for this real-life escape, however, could have come from a scene in a movie, a movie about the Berlin Wall which divides Communist Germany from West Germany.

Living in East Berlin, two young East German college students decided they wanted freedom. What kept them from it was "The Wall."

It was the spring of 1983. They had spent months planning and preparing for their escape and collecting the equipment they would need for it: some heavy fishing line, a strong metal cable, two metal "glides" — and a bow and arrow!

When everything was ready, they sneaked to the top of a high building near the wall. Tying the cable down to anchor it, they attached it to the fishing line, and then attached the other end of the fishing line to the arrow. Next, they fired the arrow down across the border — over the wall — to some West German friends who had agreed to help them.

Barbed wire, searchlights and East German soldiers, trained to shoot on sight, were their obstacles.

Catching the line, their friends anchored it at the other side.

With the metal "glides" positioned to protect their hands, they were ready. Like movie stuntmen, the two students slid down the wire, one after the other — right over the heads of the border guards — to freedom!

Solo Sail

Naomi James was alone on her 53-foot-long sailboat, the *Express Crusader,* when it capsized in a violent, howling gale in the Pacific Ocean. Fearing for her life, she clung to the *Crusader's* hull, using strength she did not know she had. But how much longer could she hold on? How much longer before her grip was ripped loose and she was swallowed up by the ocean?

Naomi James was 2,000 miles from land!

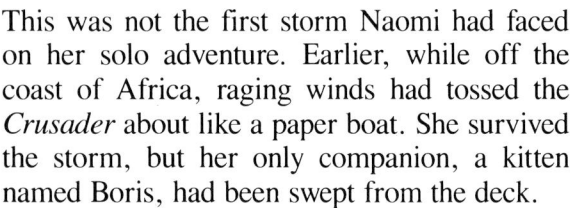

This was not the first storm Naomi had faced on her solo adventure. Earlier, while off the coast of Africa, raging winds had tossed the *Crusader* about like a paper boat. She survived the storm, but her only companion, a kitten named Boris, had been swept from the deck.

She knew how quickly the ocean could turn from soothing friend to angry beast, and although she treated it with the greatest respect, she knew it could not be trusted. With this always in mind, she thought she was prepared for the worst. What she hadn't fully realized was that there would be moments when even the greatest preparation would not help. Never in her wildest nightmares could she have imagined a greater sense of helplessness.

Although her adventure had formally begun on September 9, 1977, it really started two years earlier when she met her husband, Rob James. While the New Zealand woman had always been a "landlubber" — one prone to seasickness — her husband was an experienced sailor who loved the taste of the salty ocean air. Watching the skill with which he maneuvered his vessel over the waves, Naomi wished she could share the sense of freedom that comes with sailing — from shore it invited her, beckoned her. Swallowing her fears, Naomi made a brave decision: she wanted to share this interest. She had to learn how to sail!

Glad of her choice, James taught her all he knew and Naomi, once having conquered her seasickness, was a quick learner. Although a person can't become a skilled sailor overnight, Naomi's eagerness sped her along, and after only a few months, she had decided to sail around the world — alone.

Her husband encouraged her, but there was much more for Naomi to learn. Together they concentrated on polishing her seamanship and, with the days and hours, her confidence grew.

Countless other preparations were needed for the 30,000-mile trip, but at last she was ready to go; just her, 200 books, maps and charts, food and water, the kitten, Boris, and stacks of cassette music tapes for the long, quiet hours at sea.

Later, she admitted she was not as prepared for the trip as she might have been. Her navigational skills, at the start, were not good. But she improved.

She recounts: "I spent the first few months confusing latitude and longitude."

By the time she finally had it all straightened out, it didn't really matter that much anymore, she said, ". . . because I'd already navigated halfway around the world."

But her navigational problems had nothing to do with her current problem.

The *Express Crusader*, on which she'd known countless hours of peace and solitude, this boat which had over the months become her home, now offered her little security. How terribly small it seemed against the blackness of endless ocean, its deck and mast submerged in foam. Naomi gulped for air with the crashing of every wave, believing death was her next step. Nothing short of a miracle could save her.

And then it happened . . . slowly, at first, the mast rose. Naomi hung on, not believing her eyes. Within seconds, the boat righted itself, popping out of the water that had almost become her grave.

Later, she said it was the blackest day of the 272-day voyage, an adventure that made her the first woman to sail around the world by herself.

There had been other problems she'd encountered over the months, but loneliness, she said, wasn't one of them. She's a loner, she admits, and "I don't miss people generally." Of a cruise to the West Indies with friends she said, "Cruising with other people wasn't nearly so enjoyable as doing it on my own."

Everest's First Woman

Sir Edmund Hillary had a rough and dangerous time becoming the first man to reach the top of Mount Everest, the world's highest mountain. It was no less easy for Junks Tabei, the first woman to make the climb.

As part of a Japanese Ladies Expedition in 1975, she embarked on the journey of endurance up the 5.4-mile Mount Everest.

Although 22 years had passed since Hillary's famous ascent, the great mountain — known to Tibetans as Oomolangma, "the world's mother goddess" — had not softened her greeting to visitors. Her winds were still strong enough to literally "blow you away," and the Japanese expedition carried ice screws in their packs to anchor their tents by night. Unpredictable, her slopes were known for cave-ins and avalanches; it was as though the great Mount Everest used every device possible to keep intruders from reaching her top. Everest's crown, the highest spot on earth, could be conquered only by the strongest willed and the most determined.

Junks Tabei's expedition climbed to within 4,000 feet of the summit with only the normal problems of high-altitude climbing. They knew their luck had thus far been good — perhaps too good — and so, when they heard the rumbling of an avalanche, they'd almost expected this terror of terrors!

Tons of snow and rocks tumbled down the mountainside, injuring nearly all of the women, including Tabei. Some were forced to quit the climb. They turned to begin their descent down the mountain, but Tabei refused to leave. Hurt or not, she would go on.

As the remaining climbers rose yet higher, they suffered from severe oxygen depletion, and this, combined with their injuries, decided their journey's end. They all turned back, except for the one determined woman.

Ultimately, Tabei and Ang Tsring, a Sherpa guide, reached the mountain's summit and, as the first woman to reach the mother goddess' crown, Tabei made history.

NORTH POLE

Once Christopher Columbus proved that the world was round and shaped like a ball — instead of flat and shaped like a pancake — it was only a matter of time before people started dreaming about standing on the very top of it. One such person was Robert Edwin Peary.

The American explorer knew how hard reaching the Pole would be because he'd spent years in the Arctic as a member of numerous scientific and exploratory expeditions. Thirteen years before, he'd traveled inland over the Greenland ice sheet for 100 miles, reaching a point of 7,500 feet above sea level, and nine years later, in 1891, he returned there with seven others, including his wife, to prove that Greenland was an island and not just a field of ice. All this time the idea to be the first to reach the Pole had been brewing in his mind, and in 1894 he made his first attempt — and met with his first failure.

A second attempt was made in 1905. On a specially designed ship, *The Roosevelt*, Peary sailed as far as Cape Sheriden, Ellesmere Island, but unusually severe weather conditions made sledging his way to the Pole impossible, and he reached only as far as 87 degrees north. But Peary was not a man to give up. Obsessed with being the first to the world's top and with planting the U.S. flag there, he returned to try again in 1908.

Years of planning and raising money had gone into the quest of his Arctic dream, as well as tons of provisions and equipment and several hundred sled dogs. His years spent studying the "Arctic Highlanders" — an isolated Eskimo tribe — turned out to be invaluable. Among these Eskimos he'd found friends who helped him on many of his Arctic expeditions, and their teachings were essential to the success of the great Pole excursion.

Despite the preparations, the obstacles were countless. Temperatures of more than 50 degrees below zero and gale-like winds made frostbite and snow blindness a constant danger. Their biggest problem was the Arctic Ocean itself; most of the ice in the Arctic covers water, not land, and at any moment the ice can crack, leaving long, wide, river-sized expanses of freezing water! When this happens, explorers are trapped, cut off from the rest of their team. Worse, they could be plunged into a freezing death if a crack opened beneath their feet.

With his first try of 1894 behind him, Peary knew all this, and banking on his experience, he knew he would not be defeated by the North Pole again. He had planned for every possible emergency. He was ready for anything the Arctic could do to them.

At a point about 400 miles from the Pole, Peary, with his team — including Matthew Henson, a black companion who had been with Peary on every polar expedition since 1887 — established his base camp.

The rest of the trip would be made by dogsled and skis — and a lot of walking.

As well, there would be waiting.

When their route was severed by a wide break in the ice that had filled with water, the days of waiting seemed endless. Peary described it in his book *The North Pole* in 1910:

"Three, four, five days passed in intolerable inaction, and still the broad line of black water spread before us . . . "During those five days I paced back and forth, deploring the luck which, when everything else was favorable, should thus impede our way with open water."

Peary and his team spent a month traveling 280 miles — less than 10 miles a day. By the time they were 133 miles from the Pole, Peary had sent almost all of the team members back to base camp because of exhaustion.

Only Peary, Henson and four Eskimos would make the final lunge for the top. They would do it in a series of five forced marches which meant traveling twice as fast as they'd done on their first days when they were fresh and rested. Their magnetic compasses useless at that latitude, they navigated themselves by the position of the sun and stars until finally, almost miraculously, they walked their last mile.

On April 6, 1909, they reached the North Pole. Peary described how he felt:

"The Pole at last! The prize of three centuries. My dream and goal for twenty years. Mine at last!"

Easier Ways to the Top

Reaching the North Pole can be either dangerous or easy.

Today, people can travel to the Pole as tourists!

Some travel agencies will arrange to take you there. While some companies merely fly you over the Pole, others land so that everyone can get out and have his picture taken standing on top of the world!

The U.S. Navy's first atomic submarine, *The Nautilus*, sailed underneath the site on August 3, 1955, with the crew sitting warm and comfortable inside.

In 1978, Naomi Ueura, a Japanese adventurer, became the first man to walk to the Pole alone, accompanied only by his sled and dogteam.

Facing many of the hardships of the earlier explorers — storms, freezing temperatures and the constant threat of being trapped by broken ice — he had, as well, the nearly fatal experience of encountering a polar bear. The one thing he didn't worry about was food and other basics. At regular intervals a plane parachuted supplies to him. In 55 days, he reached his goal.

Double Eagle II

In the gondola of their helium balloon, Ben Abruzzo shivered constantly. For nearly three days it had been raining; he was soaked through to his bones, but this was the least of his worries. Trapped in a cyclone, they were floating dangerously low, only 2,000 feet above the frigid Atlantic waves — and they were sinking fast! Seeing that their journey was bound downwards, Maxie radioed for help.

Ben Abruzzo and Maxie Anderson crashed off the coast of Iceland, very nearly adding their names to the list of five others who had died trying to cross the Atlantic in a balloon. They were spared this dubious distinction by a speedy rescue team which fished them from the freezing water and allowed them a second chance.

A year later, in 1978, there was a new balloon: the eleven-story high *Double Eagle II*. Maxie Anderson and Ben Abruzzo would try again. This time, a third man, Larry Newman, would join them.

Liftoff of the *Double Eagle II* was nearly three hours behind schedule, so when they rose into the sky from Presque Isle, Maine, dusk was soon upon them. It was August 11. In less than a week they would hope to touch the ground of France, near Paris.

By their second day they flew over Newfoundland and all was running perfectly. Once, they had suddenly dropped 3,500 feet, but by their experience of the year before, they knew the worst thing they could do was panic. This time they kept calm, threw only a little of their ballast weight overboard . . . and rose again.

Wrapped in woolens and wearing oxygen masks, at 16,500 feet, the crew noticed that ice was forming on the balloon. Again they began to drop, and again they had to caution themselves against overreacting. Rather than panic and throw valuable ballast overboard, they hoped they could wait the few hours until morning. When the sun rose brightly, hundreds of pounds of ice that had weighed them down melted into a shower of rain, but their smiles and sighs of relief were stopped short — there, in their path, was a storm!

They watched anxiously as the storm veered north. The three men cheered when the sun broke through the clouds and the skies cleared. They were at 23,500 feet and could see clear sailing on a good wind — but, suddenly, they noticed they'd begun to drop again!

A large cloud hanging directly overhead blocked the sun's heat, and in the coolness of its shade, the helium of the balloon was contracting. They were falling — rapidly! They had to make a decision fast!

They didn't have much ballast left, and if they threw it all over now, they'd never have enough weight to make it to Europe! Throwing ballast over would keep them up, but when the cloud did leave, as it had to sometime, they'd be so light that they'd shoot up like a rocket! They'd keep soaring higher and higher. At 29,000 feet their balloon was designed to automatically deflate much of its helium — that would drop them right back down again! There'd be no going up after that.

It was not easy to tell themselves not to panic. It seemed that whatever they did would cause their "downfall." Either way, they were doomed to crash, and it was only a question of now or later.

They had to keep some ballast, they decided, which meant they would only throw some — not all — overboard. They threw just enough to cut the speed of the fall by half — but they were still dropping. Larry was worried. Even after they'd stabilized, they were still riding dangerously low, He bet $100 that they would not rise again above 12,500 feet. When just half an hour later they rose above that point, he happily threw the money at his companions!

On day five of the trip they received a radio transmission that they were over Ireland. They had made it! They had crossed the Atlantic! But tired as they were, their success didn't dawn on them until the next day, when they saw the wide, green fields of France below.

When they floated down onto a farmer's field just outside Paris, thousands of cheering people rushed forward to greet them. The *Double Eagle II* had landed!

Treasure of Slot ter Hooge

More than 200 years ago, in 1724, the sails of the gallant new ship, *Slot ter Hooge*, billowed white against a blue sky as she left her Netherlands port. Her hull laden with riches, she was en route to the Dutch East Indies on a trading mission when, off the coast of Portugal, a violent gale smashed her against the rocks and she sank. John Lethbridge, an expert diver of his day, was hired to retrieve the lost treasure. With his "diving machine" — a wooden barrel in which he could descend to 60 feet — Lethbridge managed, amazingly, to recover more than half of the precious hold. But hundreds of silver bars and other untold riches remained on the inlet floor of Port Santo.

In May of 1975, a veteran treasure hunter, Robert Stenuit, arranged an expedition to find *Slot ter Hooge's* remaining treasure. After much researching and poring over old and yellowed maps, Stenuit and four other divers began their search.

One day near the end of summer, when Stenuit had remained on shore, the other divers combed the inlet floor with the underwater vacuum machine known as an "airlift." Suddenly, an odd clunking sound came from the airlift and, to the joy of the treasure hunters, it turned out to be a large silver bar! Nearly thirty more bricks were found, a few at a time, but it wasn't until September that Louis, one of the divers, swam over to Stenuit, waving frantically for him to follow. There, half buried beneath seaweed and sand, was a decayed chest full of silver!

Before it was touched or moved, Stenuit wanted the chest photographed, just as it had been found. But when an underwater cameraman arrived a few days later, and they returned to the site — the treasure was gone!

Stenuit cursed himself for leaving the treasure unguarded, but immediately set out to find the guilty party. After a long ordeal, the "pirates" — a group of young divers from the nearby Madeira Islands — were discovered and forced to return the stolen treasure.

But Stenuit did not leave prospective treasure hunters with nothing. Like John Lethbridge had more than 200 years before, Stenuit left behind some of the precious hold for other hunters of the sea. Some hundred silver bars remain yet to be uncovered off the coast of Porto Guilherme.

In Search of the Yeti

The people who live on Mount Everest, the world's tallest mountain, have their own name for it: "The Mother Goddess of the World." And, as they know, the Mother Goddess has some frightening children living with her — the Yeti!

Legends of the Yeti, or Abominable Snowman, have haunted the Himalayas for centuries. Claimed to be seven feet tall, they are dark and furry humanoids who lurk in the high mountain passes of Tibet. To mention the Yeti is enough to set most mountain people trembling. But who had ever caught one? Who had any evidence? Who had seen them? Sir Edmund Hillary, the first ever to climb Mount Everest, was one of the many who wanted to find out.

An earlier visit in 1952 had whetted Hillary's curiosity. While in the Himalayan Mountains, his party discovered a strange-looking tuft of black hair. Hillary wanted to take it for examination, but the natives, wide-eyed with fear, threw it over a cliff.

In 1960, Hillary returned, leading an expedition of scientists and adventurers from the U.S.A., New Zealand, Great Britain, India, Nepal and Australia. Each of these people, like Hillary, shared a deep interest in the Yeti. Some even claimed to have had what they thought were encounters with the wild men, but none knew for sure.

Tales of the Yeti could be found everywhere. The Himalayans were full of stories and eager to tell them. They enjoyed nothing better, it seemed, than hearing a spine-chilling tale, half frightening themselves out of their wits. They'd heard the Yeti, they said, prowling around their tents at night!

Several Yeti scalps were produced, the bones from a Yeti hand, and even a complete Yeti skin! As well, Hillary and his scientists found footprints — very large, humanlike footprints.

Now it was time to apply some 20th century science to an old legend.

Investigation showed the prints to be only animal prints that had partially melted in the sunlight, then reformed into "Yeti prints." The "Yeti hand" was also a disappointment. Kept as a relic in a Tibetan monastery in Pangboche, it turned out to be a human hand with several animal bones joined to it. And the scalps, too, were phony; made many years earlier from animal skins, they had been dried out and stretched to form large pointed caps.

The prize possession of the Himalayan village of Beoring, the "Yeti skin" was, after all, only the skin of the rare Tibetan Blue Bear.

Following a year of seeking proof, Hillary had to believe that the Yeti lived only in legend.

The Himalayans, however, could not be convinced so easily. Although the "evidence" — the scalps, the hand and the skins — were shown to be faked, the Himalayans *knew* the Yeti lived. They knew it, their fathers had known it, and their fathers' fathers had known it — and very likely, their children would know it, too. And perhaps, some of them would see it . . . perhaps one day the scientists and the great adventurers would have their proof — if the Yeti were not too wise for them.

In 1985, 25 years later, an educated man named Guo, who had worked in Tibet for ten years, disagreed strongly with Hillary's conclusion.

As recently as 1979, says Guo, the Yeti had been encountered, and he has no doubt whatsoever of their existence. Guo and two other Chinese officials lived at that time in a mountainside hut in Tibet. On this particular evening, Guo left his friends alone, and so, although he did not see the Yeti himself, his colleagues' story convinced him. They claim that while they slept a hairy, manlike creature entered their hut, waking one of the men when it touched his face. "He thought it was his friend playing a joke . . ." said Guo, "then he realized it" — the hand — "was furry." The man's screams woke his companion, and the two men wrestled the creature to the floor. Then, with rope, they bound it tightly. When they dozed off during the night, however, it was all the time needed for the Yeti to escape, and when the men rose from their slumber the following morning — the creature was gone!

Virunga's Mountain Gorillas

High in the Virunga Mountains of Central Africa, where the clouds hang low in a thick, white mist, live the largest apes on the planet. These black, hulking creatures weigh up to 400 pounds; their strength and ferociousness have long been the subject of campfire tales, and just their mention chills the spine of the bravest Virunga native. When Dian Fossey, a small dark-haired woman, cut her trail up the mountainside in search of the great apes, many thought that was the last they would ever see of her.

She wanted to study the gorillas, but in such a way that her own presence would not affect their behavior. The best way to do this, she decided, was to act like a gorilla.

Climbing up into the branches of large trees, she watched — but not quietly. She'd discovered very early in her studies that one of the quickest ways to gain acceptance from gorillas was to imitate their sounds. By doing so, she could blend in with their voices and sometimes she would even start a "vocalization" which they would answer. She watched how they acted, their body movements, gestures and scratching, and these she copied as faithfully as she could.

For three years, from 1969 to 1971, Dian observed them, each day seeking them out, following them, then hiking back to her little camp. During this time she came to know the gorillas as individuals — each with his or her own character — and when it came time to leave the Virunga Mountains, Dian felt she was parting from friends. The African mountain gorilla, for so long feared, was in Dian's eyes one of the gentlest creatures of the animal kingdom.

Heyerdahl's Tigris

Thor Heyerdahl and his crew were prepared for danger when they set out on their sea trek through the Persian Gulf and Arabian Sea. They were attempting to make a journey in modern times with a boat designed thousands of years ago — the "ancient" reed ship *Tigris*.

They were prepared for the storms and other hazards that the ancient sailors would have faced. But they hadn't bargained for the danger that lurked in the present.

The adventurers, a crew of eleven men from nine different countries, were attempting to re-create and trace the 5,000-year-old trade route from Egypt and the Middle East to Africa, a route that was used by Sumerian traders back in 3500 BC. To do it, they built a boat just like the ones used by the ancient Sumerians. The *Tigris* measured 60 feet long and 20 feet across at its widest point, and was made of reeds which were tied into bundles by Arab craftsmen. Scientists had always claimed that no boat could have been seaworthy enough to travel such distances 5,000 years ago, but with this "reed boat," the *Tigris,* Heyerdahl wanted to prove them wrong.

They called the boat *Tigris* in honor of their starting point — a place where the Tigris River meets the Euphrates River. According to many people, the land there is the actual Garden of Eden.

For good fortune, although Heyerdahl objected to it, the natives sacrificed six sheep to the ancient gods and anointed the hull with their bloody handprints. Later, when a near fatal accident hindered the boat's smooth launching, some of the Arabs insisted that the gods were angry because Heyerdahl had refused to allow the sacrifice of a bull.

The ancient sailors, however, did not have to share the oceans with the giant oil tankers that make the Indian Ocean and the Arabian Sea so crowded today.

Sailing the *Tigris* through the Indian Ocean and the Arabian Sea was like riding a bicycle on an expressway filled with giant speeding trucks during a rainstorm.

Whenever Heyerdahl and his crew were in the major shipping lanes, which was often, they had to be on guard constantly. Their boat was only 60 by 20 feet (the size of a house), while many of the oil tankers were well over three football fields long, more than 200 feet wide! An oil tanker can weigh more than 30,000 fully grown elephants! What's more, since the *Tigris* was made of reeds and wood, it couldn't be detected on radar. At night or when it rained, they were almost invisible to passing ships.

It was up to the *Tigris* crew to spot the oil tankers and get out of their way — or be crushed! In one instance, a giant oil tanker passed so close that they could smell the diesel fumes and feel the heat from the ship's engines!

Besides avoiding the great steel hulls of tankers and freighters, they faced another problem: water pollution. Huge oil slicks and other patches of foul-smelling water stretched over the ocean's surface, slowing their path. Such sights appeared ugly and discouraged the crew, not just because of their own travel, but because they knew pollution was permanently harming the ocean, killing plant and wildlife.

Although the *Tigris* was no match for the giant vessels, during a storm the reed boat fared

beautifully! The *Tigris'* reed hull was stable and flexible, giving easily with the waves. The reeds, unlike wooden planks or metal, acted like a sieve so that the waves, however violent, passed through them with little harm. On deck was another story — one storm was so severe it tore the mast and sail from the boat! Crew members had to tie themselves with tethers to keep from being swept overboard!

Still, Heyerdahl had no doubts that the reed ships of the Sumerians would have been perfectly designed for long-distance travel; in fact, the *Tigris* was better adapted to the wild ways of the sea than many of its modern counterparts.

After three months, having survived many dangers, they approached their final destination — the coast of Africa. A continent of turmoil at the time, its countries raging with war, a final danger to the *Tigris* group was being mistaken as the enemy. A bullet or bomb fired accidentally at them could easily destroy them. Radio transmissions warned them against docking. This happened port after port.

Only one African nation would permit them to come ashore.

That was Djibouti, at the head of the Gulf of Aden. After 144 days and 4,200 miles on what was, in effect, a 5,000-year-old boat, they'd more than proven their point! They'd not only coped with all that the ancient sailors had faced, but they had survived the hazards of a modern world!

SOUTH POLE

The main reason Norway's Roald Amundsen became the first man to stand on the very bottom of the world was that the U.S.'s Robert Peary had beaten him to the top of it.

It wasn't until Amundsen and his team sailed from Norway that he told them they wouldn't be going north. Since he couldn't be the first to go to the North Pole, he'd be the first to the South Pole!

His crew agreed.

The challenges facing them would, in some ways, be even rougher than the one Peary had faced. As cold as the North Pole is, the South Pole is colder. A steady and frigid west wind blows across its frozen surface at an average speed of 50 miles an hour, and gales of more than 100 miles an hour are common!

A final challenge was a British team who were headed for the same destination. Led by British Navy Captain Robert Scott — another veteran Arctic and Antarctic explorer — the British team had a head start on the Norwegians.

Amundsen wasn't worried. He sent Scott a telegram to let him know he was racing to the Pole.

On January 9, 1911, the Norwegians reached Antarctica where they spent ten months performing scientific tests and making preparations for the actual polar lunge. It would be the beginning of spring before they would begin their march.

Spring in the Antarctic is not a time of green leaves and blossoms. It is a desolate land of cruel temperatures and bitter conditions.

Eight sled dogs died almost immediately, victims of the harsh weather. Later, the expedition was forced to kill 24 more that were too weak to go on. Drained of their strength, the sled dogs cowered like puppies, and collapsing exhausted on the snow, they awaited their end. When a major gale hit, wild winds swept the barren land into a white turmoil. With the snow flying, it was impossible to tell where the land ended and the sky began.

The force of the blizzard sucked the breath from their lungs, and the explorers strained with every step. At last, they fell to their hands and knees, dragging themselves over the ice. They could not go on.

Their fingers blistered from the cold, they drove spikes into the ice to keep their tents from ripping loose and crawled inside. Like prisoners, they were trapped! Minutes dragged into hours and hours into days, and still the gale raged madly. Around the dim light of their oil lamps, the men's eyes, red-rimmed from exhaustion, searched each other for an answer. They could not wait forever. Scott and his British team might even now be approaching the Pole, and they could not just sit and allow him to get there first.

On the fifth day, with the gale still screaming, the explorers decided to move on. They would rather risk death than spend any more time waiting, for the worst thing that could happen would be to reach the South Pole only to find the English flag flying over it.

Finally, they were only a day's march away. Despite the frostbite and constant biting wind, they were eager. Amundsen later wrote: "The atmosphere of the tent that night was like the eve of some great festival."

On December 14, 1911, they reached the South Pole. After only four days they turned homeward, leaving a letter there for Scott.

In his later years, Amundsen wrote about being the first one to reach the South Pole instead of the North Pole.

"I had better be honest and admit straight out that I had never known any man to be placed in such a diametrically opposite position to the goal of his desires as I was at that moment. The regions around the North Pole — well, yes, the North Pole itself — have attracted me from childhood and here I stood at the South Pole. Can anything more topsy turvy be imagined?"

ROBERT SCOTT

Robert Scott first saw Antarctica in 1901 as part of a scientific expedition. The cold, desolate land of the far south fascinated the British naval officer, and over the years he grew to cherish a dream of being the first man to reach the South Pole.

In 1911 Scott formed an Antarctic expedition. Its purpose was to make that dream reality — to plant the British flag at the South Pole. A telegram from Roald Amundsen challenging him to a race to the Pole didn't worry him. Scott's team had already left; they had a head start.

Though months had been spent in preparation for the trip, one can never be fully prepared for the Antarctic. After a long, dangerous and physically exhausting march, most of the explorers were unable to continue. Scott sent them back to base camp and decided, with the four who remained, to brave the last 175 miles.

When finally, after months of anguish, the South Pole came into view, the men stopped in their tracks. Disbelief and an agony worse than they'd yet experienced clutched at their throats. Could it be? Could it really be that they'd been beaten?

The Norwegian flag flapped in the wind. It was no mirage. Amundsen had won the race!

Crushed with disappointment, the five men started back.

Months later, searchers found Scott's frozen body and two others. The bodies of the other two men were never recovered. Also discovered was Scott's diary. His last entry was dated March 28, 1912:

"We shall stick it out to the end but we are getting weaker, of course, and the end cannot be far. It seems a pity but I do not think I can write anymore."

Man on the Moon

Despite the assistance of millions of dollars worth of equipment, the best computer and communications gear in the world, and a full backup staff on earth, U.S. astronauts Neil Armstrong, Edwin Aldren and Michael Collins were more on their own than any men had every been before.

Like the earliest explorers who braved the sea on rafts, the three astronauts were alone in space, relying only on their training, experience and a thin shell of modern technology; in an environment where the tiniest leak or malfunction could mean death.

Death in space can be instantaneous. Even worse, it can be slow and lingering. Their dying words might be heard by millions of people on earth who would be unable to help them.

To millions of people around the world who watched and listened to the *Apollo II* spaceflight, the most nerve-racking moment was not at takeoff, when the great rocket flashed and rumbled and shook the earth. The most gripping moment was when the rocket slipped silently behind the moon.

Aside from their equipment, the biggest safety device the crew of the *Apollo II* had was their radio; they were in constant touch with Houston. Everything that happened, everything that might happen, was being analyzed by the astronauts in space and by teams of the best scientific and technical experts on earth.

Their radio was their lifeline . . . and it was about to be cut!

Before they could land on the moon, they would have to orbit it, traveling around its dark side. Once the moon was between their tiny ship and the home planet, all radio communications would be blocked, and it was at this point — behind the moon — that the *Apollo II* would release its lunar module, rocketing two of its astronauts to the moon's surface.

The *Apollo II* was made up of three basic modules: *The Columbia* or command module, where the three astronauts rode; the service module, which held the power plant and systems needed for flight; and the *Eagle*, in which two of the astronauts would descend to the moon. While cut off from communication with earth, Neil Armstrong and Edwin Aldren would climb into the *Eagle* while Collins remained in the command module to fire his companions into orbit. Collins would "burn" or fire retrorockets to set up the *Eagle's* orbit for the lunar landing. If he failed, or if anything else went wrong on the dark side of the moon, the two men in the *Eagle* would never see earth again.

The world held its breath until the rocketship became visible. Then, there was rejoicing! Collins reported that the burn ". . . was perfect — it was like perfect."

That maneuver had put them into the proper orbit for the next phase — landing. Once the lunar lander, the *Eagle*, had separated from the command module which Collins would keep in space, all was A-OK.

The *Eagle* landed on the moon on July 20, 1969. Hours later, a quarter of a million miles away on the planet earth, millions of people watching on TV saw Neil Armstrong climb down the *Eagle's* ladder. He became the first man in history to set foot on another planetary body.

While no one knows what the first words spoken by the first person to discover North America were, we do know the first words spoken by the first person to walk on the moon:

"That's one small step for man, one giant leap for mankind."

Many people consider the landing of the *Apollo II* to be the end of an adventure, an adventure that had really started with the first person who looked up at the moon and wondered if it were possible to get there.

Others, however, consider it just the start of one.

If you watch *Star Trek,* you hear the words:

"Space, the final frontier."

That final frontier is waiting to be explored. The space adventure is just beginning.

FLYING MACHINE

Comic books and science-fiction stories have been describing people flying in space for years; not just with rocketships, but independently, with jetpacks on their backs.

U.S. astronaut Bruce McCandless, and others, had been working on a real-life jet-powered backpack for ten years. At last, in February of 1984, McCandless was going to see if it worked.

On board the U.S. space shuttle *Challenger*, McCandless put on the special jet backpack, stepped out of the cargo bay door and faced the vast emptiness of outer space — 180 miles above earth. He disconnected the lifeline that kept him safely attached to the space shuttle, turned on his jets and shot off into space. McCandless became the first person ever to float in space untethered, unattached to anything!

"This is neat. We sure have a nice flying machine here," McCandless radioed to the space shuttle crew and the anxious people on earth. And remembering the words of U.S. astronaut Neil Armstrong when he became the first man to step on the moon, he said, "It might have been one small step for Neil, but it was a giant leap for me."

Family Trip

The Bushnills view adventuring as both a family project and a way of life. The fact that their way of life could get them killed doesn't discourage them — danger is part of the price paid for adventure. Even after seven years of traveling strange and sometimes wild oceans, they don't consider that price too high.

Winston Bushnill, his wife Carolynne and their daughters, Kim and Leslie, of Sudbury, Ontario, Canada, began a project in their backyard. After months of working together, nails, lumber and paint came together in the construction of a 31-foot boat. Her name was *The Dove*, and in the seven years to come, she would be their home. From her deck the Bushnills would see the world unfold around them.

Kim was ten and Leslie just eight when the adventure began in 1972. A few years later, near the Cape of Good Hope, it almost ended.

With his family below, Winston relaxed at the tiller. The sky was clear and the air calm, but on the sea, storms can strike suddenly. Winston could not have foreseen that soon they would come face to face with death!

Black clouds gathered and the wind picked up. Though great danger was not yet apparent, Winston wisely prepared for the worst. With a 60-foot line, he tethered himself to the boat, while his family remained secure inside the cabin.

The Indian Ocean is known for its nightmarish storms, and soon enough, the Bushnills were in the heart of one. The wind speed jumped to nearly 60 miles an hour and, within moments, the ocean became a raging beast, frothing with madness. *The Dove* was tossed about like a feather! When the ocean is hungry for lives, a man can do little but tremble, and so when Winston saw a giant (taller than a five-story building) wave rushing toward him, he had not even the will to scream. *The Dove*, thrust off balance, was upset and Winston was swept from her deck.

Although the black waves threatened to take him, his greatest struggle was with himself — trying not to panic. His tether, he realized, was his lifesaver. Without it he would never have managed to return to the boat. When at last he was within its range, he was glad to see she had righted herself — but there were losses.

Carolynne had two broken ribs, and the children, though not seriously hurt, were bruised and shaken. *The Dove*, too, had suffered. The cabin's hatch had been ripped loose and water had poured in. With the storm still raging around them, their luck would not change for a while — the hatch had to be refastened immediately!

Within an hour, another thunderous wave struck! Then another, and another! Four times they tipped and each time Winston was swept away. With the tether, he managed always to regain his position. Repairing the storm's damage was an ongoing task. When a porthole popped open with the force of a wave, there was no time to panic. Time spent worrying is all the time it takes to sink, and so, with furious speed and the will to survive, they succeeded in sealing it. When it happened again, they knew exactly what to do.

For eight hours this was their life — fighting for it!

For three days the gale blustered, but they'd survived the worst. However, with both masts lost and their engine disabled, they were doomed to drift aimlessly. It was five days before the crew of a passing ship found them, fed them and towed them to land.

Such dangers were to occur again, but never once did the Bushnills think of ending their voyage. Though the ocean can be a rushing beast, it also knows a peace not found in any city, and the seafarer's life, rich with the unexpected, does not return easily to the working man's day of "nine to five."

When, after seven years, they returned home, they immediately started plans for another trip. Winston explained why in a magazine interview:

"The most important thing in life to me is my personal freedom."

Through the Outback by Camel

"I wanted to see the desert; I wanted to learn about camels; I wanted to be with the Aborigines . . ." Robyn Davidson explained. These were good enough reasons, in her eyes, for braving the Australian wilderness — known to Australians as the "outback" — in a 1,700-mile journey alone through regions known only to the Aborigines and a few white settlers. To cross this harsh land, dominated by the Gibson and Great Sandy deserts, a tougher animal than a horse was needed. "Camel seemed the natural way to go," said Robyn.

Robyn began her journey from Alice Springs in April, 1977, with a caravan of four camels and a dog called Diggety. Her destination was the Indian Ocean. She learned how to command and care for her four camels, but of their wild counterparts — those camels that ran loose in the harsh lands of the outback — she knew only that they were dangerous. When, just 200 yards ahead, she saw three of these large, wild camel bulls, she remembered her camel trainer's words — *don't hesitate!*

The three bulls had their eyes on Zeleika, Robyn's female camel. Sallay, the camel trainer, had said a bull camel could and would kill her if she got in its way, and here was not one bull but three! "Keep calm, keep calm," Robyn told herself . . . "Remember what Sallay said to do."

She tied up Bub, her male camel, and sat him down so he wouldn't bolt. Her trembling fingers sought the rifle and removed it from its scabbard. Load and cock . . . raise and aim. Steady. Fire!

Three shots rang out in the desert stillness, and the three bull camels fell dead.

Although shaken by having to kill the three animals, Robyn knew she'd had no choice. Life in the desert often left one without an alternative, she found, and once, later, she had to shoot her dog Diggety after he'd eaten poison that had been left by the Aborigines for wild dogs. Suffering these losses was the price of her adventure. She would later say, ". . . I like the growth and learning processes that developed from taking chances." But Robyn knew that hand in hand with growth is often pain.

IRAN ESCAPE

They were alone in Iran, six American diplomats, fugitives with nowhere to hide. If they were discovered they knew they would be taken hostage.

The Americans had supported the Shah of Iran, and when Ayatollah Ruhollah Khomeini took his place as ruler, all Americans — especially those who worked for the U.S. government — were in danger.

The nightmare started on November 4, 1979, when a mob of militant Iranian students stormed the U.S. Embassy in Tehran and took it over. Everyone there was taken prisoner. Everyone but six diplomats who had escaped!

One of them had been working in an office outside the embassy compound and had managed to hide as soon as he heard about the takeover. Five of them, however, had been inside the compound. Through a window they saw the Iranian mob storming over the gates! One Iranian had tried to break into a nearby room, but a Marine embassy guard had forced him back!

The five diplomats huddled in a back room. Shaking with fear, they watched the alley below and waited. Hours passed like days. When finally the street grew quiet, they made a run for it.

For the next six days they lived as fugitives. Around any corner their captors could be waiting. At last, in desperation, they found the Canadian embassy. It would be only a few weeks before the sixth American arrived there.

Though the Canadians welcomed them, offering the Americans protection, they knew that they could not hide the fugitives forever. Helping the Americans would endanger their own lives. It was very likely that if the Canadian embassy was found aiding the U.S., the Canadian diplomats would be taken hostage, too. Kenneth Taylor, Canada's ambassador to Iran, had to come up with a plan.

For more than two months they hid the six Americans in their homes. The Canadians knew that as each day passed the dangers became greater. They had to get the Americans out of Iran!

But how?

The border guards were on alert. People leaving the country had their passports examined very closely. If the U.S. diplomats used their American passports, they'd be arrested immediately — but those were the only passports they had!

Taylor sent secretly coded cables to Canadian Prime Minister Joe Clark. He had an idea to help the Americans. The Prime Minister agreed to the plan.

Canada prepared six "Canadian" passports for the Americans and created false identities for each of them. The U.S. Central Intelligence Agency helped Canada forge Iranian visa stamps so the Iranians would think the people were just six more Canadians who had legally entered Iran on business. Finally, the passports and papers were sent secretly to Taylor in a diplomatic pouch.

Taylor knew that if he managed to get the Americans out of Iran, the Canadian diplomats would certainly be in trouble. So, one by one, he started to send the Canadian diplomats home. Over a period of a few weeks, all the diplomats except Taylor and three others were gone.

With their fake Canadian passports, the Americans arrived at the airport. Surely, they thought, they would be detected! As their passports were closely inspected by a uniformed official, the Americans trembled. They were certain the fear in their eyes would give them away! Then, they were allowed to pass through.

Once Taylor learned that the Americans had made it, he and the last three diplomats closed their embassy and left Iran.

It was only after all the Canadian diplomats were out of the country, and the six Americans safe, that the story was released.

ENTEBBE

They were on their way to Paris that day on June 27, 1976, but they wouldn't get there.

Aboard an Air France jetliner, 106 passengers and crew became part of a terrifying hijacking that would last a week and capture the world's attention.

Seven pro-Palestinian guerillas took over the plane shortly after it left Athens on a flight from Tel Aviv to Paris. The gunmen forced the pilot to fly to Entebbe Airport in Uganda and threatened to blow up the plane and kill the hostages unless 53 Palestinian and pro-Palestinian terrorists were released from prisons in Israel and four other countries.

The tension was unbearable. The stalemate went on for days. Then, on July 4, Israeli paratroopers swooped down on Entebbe Airport and staged a dramatic rescue attempt. With a crash, the doors and windows were kicked in and men stormed through, waving machine guns.

"Get down, friends," they shouted. "Stay down. We are here."

These saviors, led by Lt. Colonel "Yonni" Netanyahu, were swift and brave. In just 53 minutes, they took off with 102 surviving hostages.

The Highest Ski Hill in the World

If you wanted to ski down the highest ski hill in the world, where would you look to find it? On the highest mountain in the world, right?

A Japanese man, Yuichira Muira, was looking for just such a mountain. He had set the world speed-skiing record of close to 110 miles per hour and had already skied on many high mountains, such as Mount Fuji in Japan. Now, he looked to the Himalayan Mountains of Nepal for his next challenge.

There, rising to 29,028 feet above sea level, is the highest point in the world — the great Mount Everest. The Himalayan mountain, which had claimed the lives of many who tried to climb it until it was conquered by Sir Edmund Hillary, now had found a man who wanted to climb it — and then ski back down!

Men who ski in speed championships do it on special hills that have a long, flat runout at the bottom or even a hill on the other side of a valley to slow them down. The reason for this is that the skiers go so fast that their skis hardly touch the snow, and without such a runout area, it is impossible to turn or slow down.

After studying photographs of Mount Everest, Muira realized that there was no such area. In fact, there was a huge crevice at the bottom of the ski run called the Bergschrund, and to ski into that would mean certain death. Muira's solution was a parachute to catch the air; it would slow him down enough so he could regain control of his skis and stop before reaching the Bergschrund.

After more than two years of planning, raising in excess of half a million dollars, and working out expected problems, the expedition began. At the town of Katmandu, about a hundred miles from the mountain, the necessary supplies and equipment were gathered. Because a film company was to make a movie of the ski run and expedition — later to be titled "The Man Who Skied Down Everest" — their load was especially heavy. One thousand Sherpa guides — "barefoot angels" as Muira called them — were needed to manage the burden.

Muira was confident. He had trained and conditioned himself carefully, applying strict attention to his diet and making sure he got enough sleep. He studied the philosophy and training methods of the ancient samurai swordsmen who were committed to their craft and way of life. Muira tried to copy the style of Myamoto Musashi, Japan's greatest swordsman, who was born in 1584. Musashi had become so great that he challenged all swordsmen in Japan to duels. However, instead of using a sword as the others did, Musashi used two sticks, defeating over a hundred opponents. Muira would be facing death in the same way, using his wits and skill to conquer it.

In the spring of 1970, Muira's expedition left Katmandu to begin the climb up Everest. Tragedy struck when an avalanche began along an icefall. Six Sherpa guides were crushed to death by the huge blocks of ice. It would mar the early part of the expedition, and make Muira wonder if he, too, would be doomed to die.

Once the expedition reached base camp, only a few climbed toward the South Col, the point 3,000 feet below the peak of the mountain from where Muira would begin his descent. The base camp was at 17,000 feet above sea level. Above that the air begins to get so thin that oxygen is necessary to breathe properly. All along the way, Muira trained for the final run.

When they reached the South Col, Muira skied a little on some soft snow, setting an altitude record. But the intended run down the mountain would follow a path of almost solid ice. If he could not stop by the time he reached the Bergschrund, there was a very small strip of snow where he could ski through, but he was now so high up that could not even see it!

Taking a few last gulps of oxygen, Muira braced himself to go, putting his mind into the "samurai situation." He would reach 125 miles per hour in just six seconds. Muira began his heart-stopping run and built up such speed that he knew he now had no control. Strangely, he could not hear the rush of wind normally felt in speed skiing. He popping his chute, but felt no tug. The air was too thin! His chute dragged uselessly!

Muira desperately tried to maneuver, tried to find that strip of life-saving snow through the Bergschrund, but he could not get to it! Observers would remark at what a fancy, twisting run Muira was making, but, in fact, he was frantically trying to find an escape route. At last, his skis found a layer of soft snow on top of the ice. He fell and skidded to a stop just a few yards from the Bergschrund.

"Don't move!" cried a voice through the radio in his helmet.

With ropes and equipment, Sherpas inched onto the snow toward him. Glad to be alive, Muira felt like a true samurai, but, as he grabbed onto the lifeline that would pull him to safety, he knew that without the barefoot angels he would have slipped to his death.

DEEPEST DIVE

You don't have to go up to find yourself in deep space. You can find it by going down, too; down to where the sun never penetrates; down to a place that's as alien to man as any undiscovered planet might be; down to a place where the creatures are as strange as anything you might imagine in outer space; down, down, down to the bottom of the ocean!

Two men did just that on January 23, 1960. They went to the very bottom, the deepest spot in the Pacific Ocean, to a place called the Challenger Deep in the Mariana Trench. The aquanauts were U.S. Navy Lieutenant Donald Walsh and scientist Jacques Piccard. They made their trip in the *Trieste,* a deep-sea diving vessel called a bathyscaphe, invented in 1940 by Auguste Piccard, Jacques' father.

Auguste Piccard had set record heights for ballooning. In a balloon of his design, he reached a height of 55,563 feet straight up (10 miles or 16 km), and others using his design went even higher! After conquering the heights of earth's atmosphere, Auguste set about reaching the ocean's depths. Using the idea that a lighter-than-air balloon could support a gondola, he realized that a lighter-than-water float could support a cabin, and he set out to invent the bathyscaphe.

A bathyscaphe is like a submarine. Both are like a spaceship: self-contained units in which people can live. While a spaceship has to make sure its astronauts are not exposed to the airless vacuum of space, a submarine (or bathyscaphe) has to make certain its occupants are protected from the airless water and incredible pressure of the ocean's depths!

At the bottom of the Challenger Deep, the water pressure on the *Trieste* was over seven tons per square inch. That's about the same as if you held seven or ten fully grown elephants in the palm of your hand!

While the *Trieste* was making its 4-hour and 45-minute descent, the pressure was so great that one of its outside portholes cracked. If it had broken or if one of the interior portholes had cracked as well, they wouldn't even have time to drown. They would have been crushed to death first!

Despite the danger, the men kept going.

Darkness and pressure have always been the biggest barriers to sea exploration, and for that reason, the ocean has always been shrouded in mystery. Although for thousands of years we've lived by the ocean, fished it and traveled its waves, it is only in the past four decades that we've begun to map what lies beneath its surface. Tales of strange life forms, of sea monsters and giant squid have long haunted sailors' voyages, but how much was imagination and how much was fact, if any? In 1938, the "coelacanth," a fish that had swum the ocean depths as long as 300 millions years ago and was long believed extinct, was discovered alive. Scientists began to look and wonder what else lay beneath the black mystery of the ocean's waves.

World War II opened the waters to discovery. With better ocean charts and the creation and advancement of marine technology, man began to venture deeper and deeper toward the ocean floor. What he found was astounding — craters and gorges that would match the Grand Canyon, and a mountain range greater that the Himalayas, the Andes and the Rockies together! They also found, in the Pacific, what their sensors told them was the deepest spot in the world — the Mariana Trench — and the deepest part of the trench — the Challenger Deep. They knew it existed, but they had no way of "seeing" it.

When Walsh and Piccard descended deeper and further than any man had yet traveled into the ocean, mankind waited eagerly to hear what they had seen.

When they reached the bottom, they were enveloped in a dense, white cloud of sediment. This ooze was made up of thousands of years of dead plants and fish that had sunk to the bottom. When the water cleared, however, they made a great discovery. They saw a small shrimp, alive and kicking, and a flatfish swimming merrily along its way. They had found life seven miles down in the ocean, under seven tons per square inch of pressure. If life could exist there, surely it could exist anywhere in the world — maybe even anywhere in the universe!